THE GHOSTLY TALES OF FLINT

Published by Arcadia Children's Books
A Division of Arcadia Publishing
Charleston, SC
www.arcadiapublishing.com

Copyright © 2021 by Arcadia Children's Books
All rights reserved

Spooky America is a trademark of Arcadia Publishing, Inc.

First published 2021

Manufactured in the United States

ISBN 978-1-4671-9835-6

Library of Congress Control Number: 2021938369

Notice: The information in this book is true and complete to the best of our knowledge. It is offered without guarantee on the part of the author or Arcadia Publishing. The author and Arcadia Publishing disclaim all liability in connection with the use of this book.

All rights reserved. No part of this book may be reproduced or transmitted in any form whatsoever without prior written permission from the publisher except in the case of brief quotations embodied in critical articles and reviews.

All images courtesy of Shutterstock.com; p. 52 Steve Lagreca/Shutterstock.com; p. 96 Atomazul/Shutterstock.com

Spooky America

THE GHOSTLY TALES OF FLINT

ANNA LARDINOIS

Adapted from *Haunted Flint*
by Roxanne Rhoads and Joe Schipani

arcadia
CHILDREN'S BOOKS

Michigan

Flint

Table of Contents & Map Key

Introduction 3

1. Chapter 1. Horrors Beneath the Haunted Hotel 7
2. Chapter 2. The Wily Whaley Family 15
3. Chapter 3. You Will Not Follow Me Home 23
4. Chapter 4. Haunted Happenings at The Capitol Theatre 31
5. Chapter 5. (Very) Creepy Carriage Town 39
6. Chapter 6. Ghosts in the Graveyard 45
7. Chapter 7. Spooky Sightings at the Sloan Museum 53
8. Chapter 8. Exit, Stage Left 61
9. Chapter 9. Check Out Time: NEVER 67
10. Chapter 10. The Macabre Masonic Temple 75
11. Chapter 11. William, Is That You? 83
12. Chapter 12. The Home Too Comfortable to Leave 91
13. Chapter 13. A Walk Along the Flint River 97

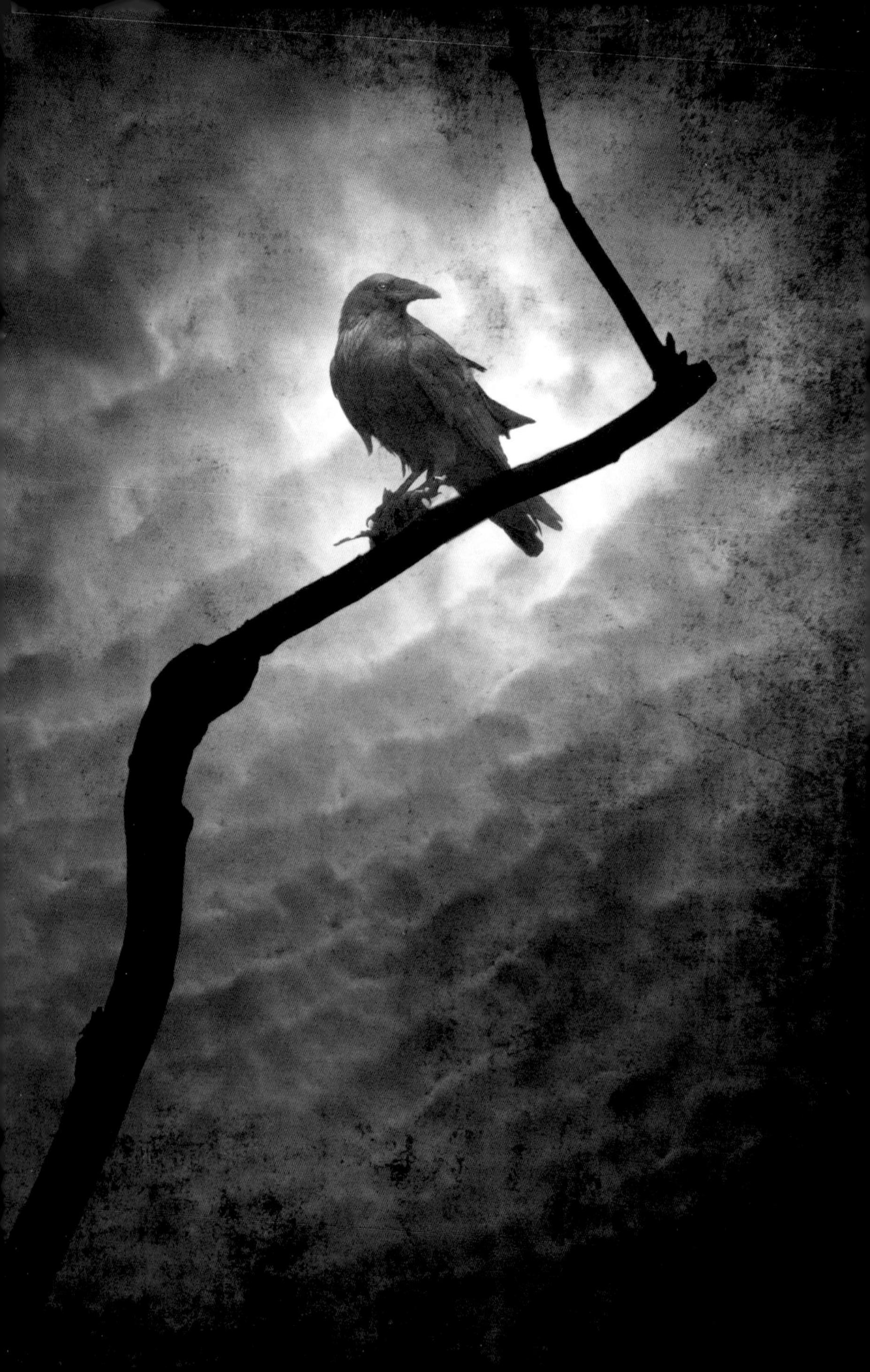

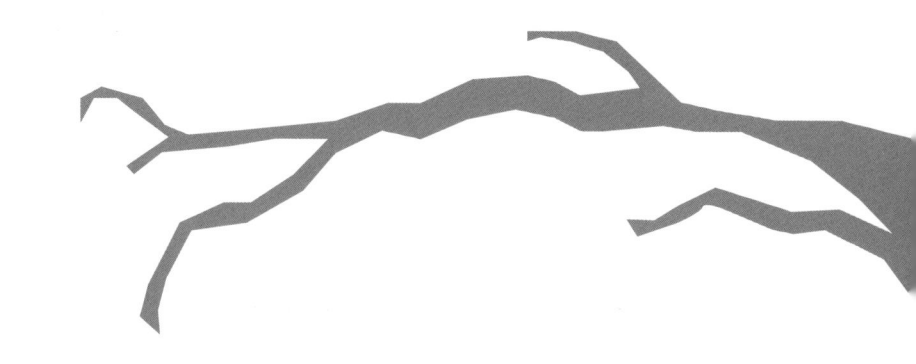

Introduction

Welcome to frightening Flint! Ever since the city was founded in 1819, Flint has been the home of some of the most industrious people in Michigan. In the early days, hardworking residents made their livings in the lumber business. Later, fortunes were made building carriages and, later still, manufacturing automobiles. The people of Flint know how to make things happen!

Flint has a long and rich history, and as you know, history comes with ghosts! These ghosts seem to be everywhere: in theaters, in museums, even walking down the street.

Introduction

Whether you are in Carriage Town, River Village, Grand Traverse Street District, or any of the other neighborhoods in Flint, chances are you have strolled by a place where people have experienced paranormal phenomena.

Flint might be known as "Vehicle City," but if you ask me, it should be known as Spooky City! Let's explore the spook-tacular side of Flint together. Just turn the page for some spine-tingling fun.

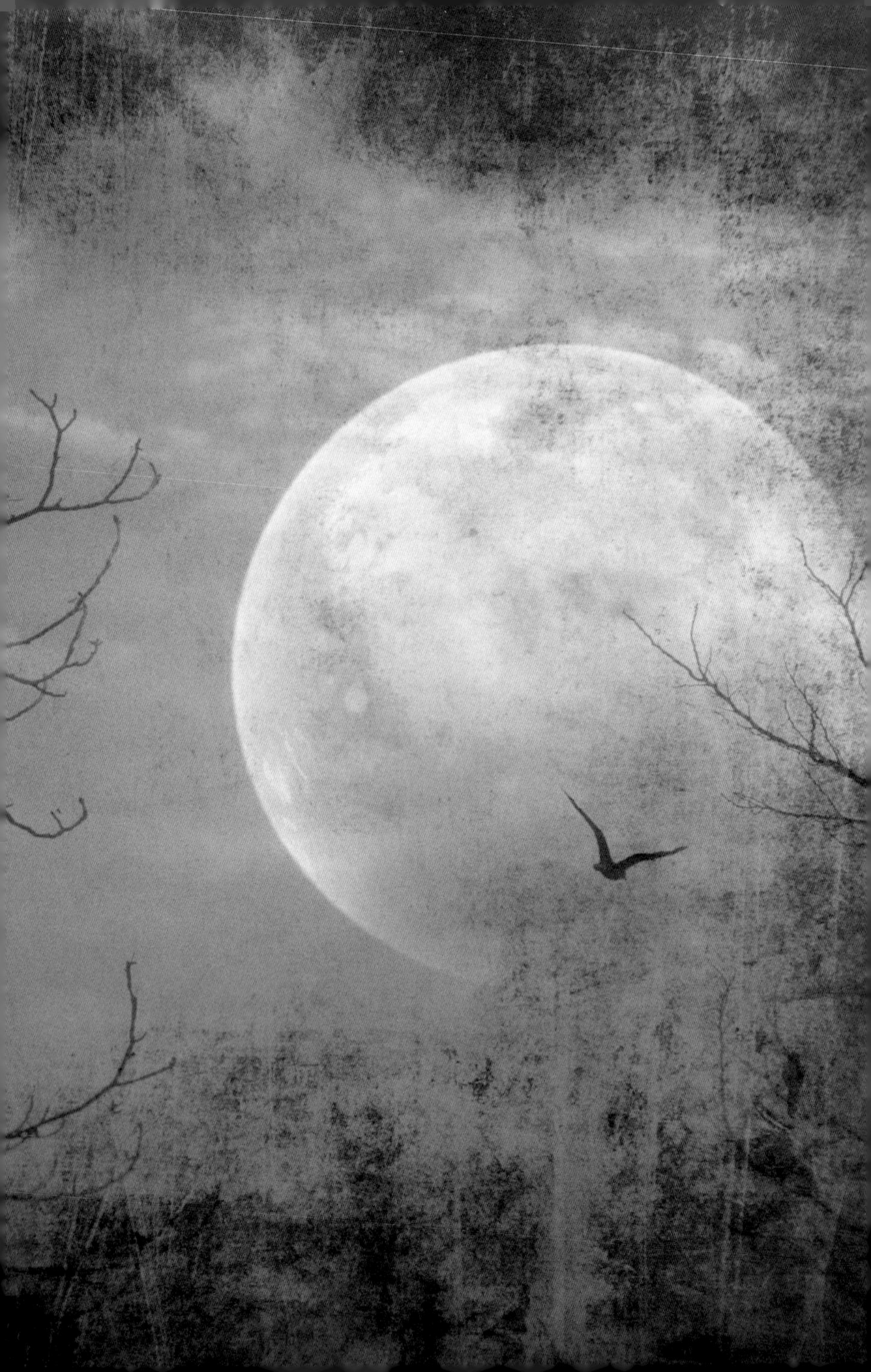

CHAPTER 1

Horrors Beneath the Haunted Hotel

How does a building become haunted? Sometimes, after a terrible event, a ghost refuses to leave the place where it took its last breath. Sometimes a plot of land itself might be cursed. Every so often, a ghost haunts a building it never even set foot inside while living. That's the case with the ghosts at The Holiday Inn Express on Robert T. Longway Boulevard and Interstate 475.

The story of this haunted hotel begins way back in 1842, when the first settlers arrived in Flint. They built a graveyard on the ground where Longway Boulevard now meets W.H. Schwartz Drive. Many of Flint's first citizens were laid to rest here. Later, it became known as the Old Flint City Cemetery.

Years passed. People moved away from the area. No one took care of Old Flint City Cemetery.

Gravestones crumbled or toppled over. Wind and rain eroded the headstones, making them hard to read. It was no longer clear who was buried where. Weeds choked out the flowers that loved ones had planted on the graves of the dead. The grass was overgrown and wild. Candy wrappers and garbage blew across the unkempt grounds. The graveyard looked sad and shabby. In fact, it looked like just the kind of place that a ghost might haunt. No one wanted to bury their loved ones in the spooky, tumbledown cemetery. People started using new cemeteries. The graveyard continued to decay. It looked spookier every year.

After many years of neglect, the city moved the dead in the Old Flint City Cemetery to the Flint City Cemetery on Linden Road and Pasadena Avenue. In 1952, a total of 1,199 of Flint's dearly departed were moved to the new graveyard. In 1958, the remaining 132,122 bodies—along with their grave markers—were moved to the Avalon Cemetery. The Old Flint City Cemetery was empty. Or at least that's what city officials THOUGHT. It would take years for them to discover how wrong they were.

After many years, a hotel was built on the land that was once the cemetery. The modern hotel had everything travelers want. There were plenty of rooms, a restaurant, and even a pool! Everything was bright, clean, and new when they opened the doors. But they were in for a BIG surprise!

Everyone was shocked in 1985 when more than two dozen bodies were found while working on the hotel's basement. Those deceased citizens, whose names were forgotten long ago, were taken to the New City Cemetery. Their caskets might have been easy to move, but their spirits didn't go quite as easily. Many believe they still linger in the hotel to this day.

Strange things happen inside the Holiday Inn Express that simply cannot be explained. Lights shut off without reason. Fully-charged electrical devices are mysteriously drained of power. Guests and employees have heard voices coming from empty hallways. Shadowy figures have been seen roaming through the building.

If that wasn't spooky enough, there are even MORE scary things that happen in this building! Hotel guests have seen doors open and close, seemingly on their own. Front desk employees report receiving telephone calls from empty hotel rooms. When they answer, no one is on the other end—at least, no one who speaks. Is it a request for room service from the other side or something more sinister?

Many believe this hotel is haunted because although the physical remains of those previously buried here were moved to a new final resting place, their spirits remain. Some believe these restless spirits are trapped here, doomed to haunt the building that was constructed over their forgotten graves.

If you go to the Holiday Inn Express to have your own ghostly adventure, be sure to stay alert! You never know what might be lurking in the hallways of the hotel. You may hope for a restful sleep in this hotel. But the restless spirits here might have other ideas. Try hanging the "Do Not Disturb" sign on your door before you turn in for the night. That *might* keep the spirits away. But, then again, it might not...

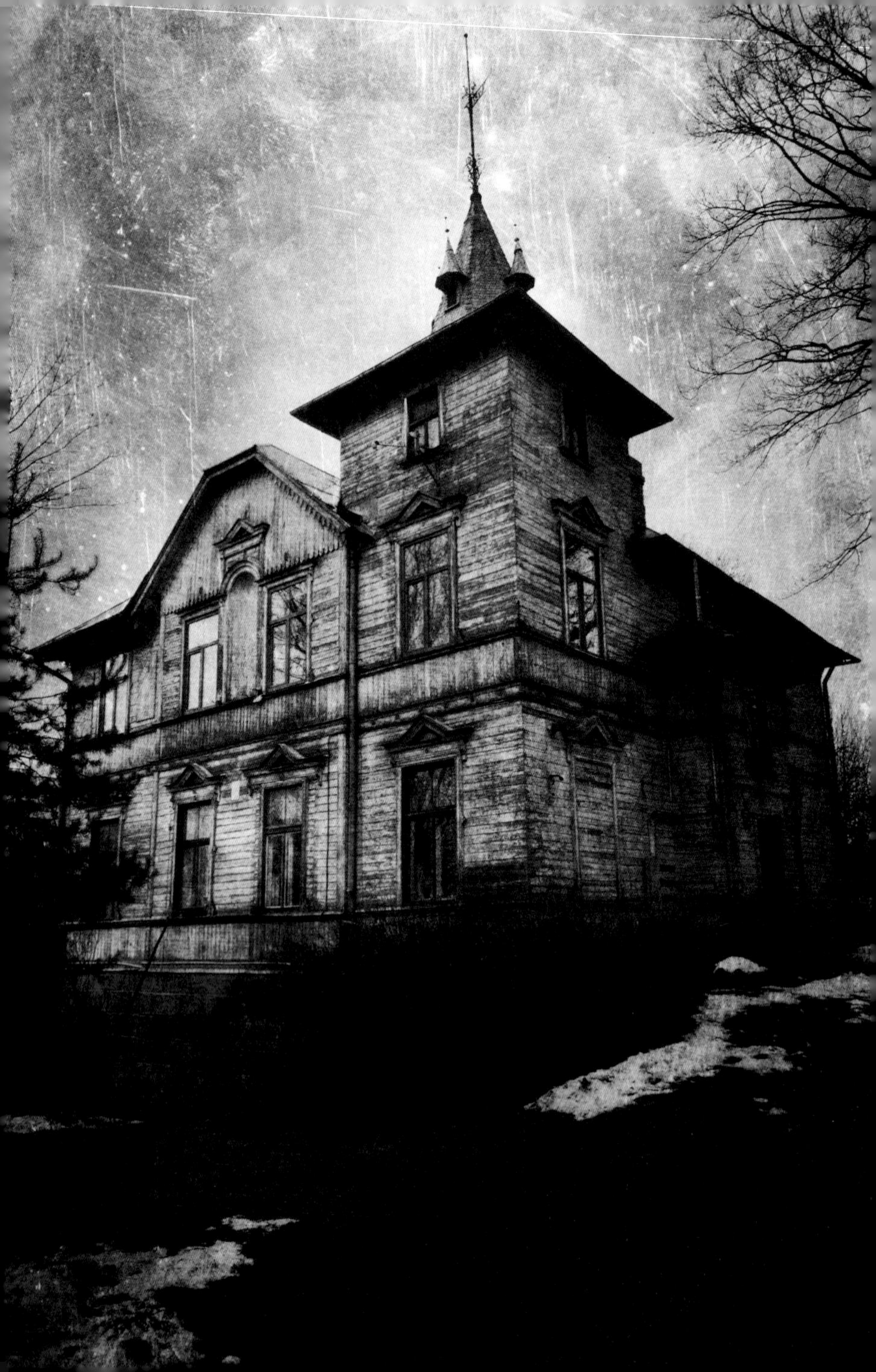

CHAPTER 2

The Wily Whaley Family

If you want to step back in time, there is no better place in Flint than at the Whaley House Museum. The grand Victorian home was built in 1859, but it became the marvelous mansion we know today in 1885, when Robert and Mary McFarlan Whaley moved into the home after completing extensive renovations.

The Whaleys were among Flint's wealthiest families. Robert was the president of Citizens

Bank at the height of Flint's business boom. The couple shared the home with their daughter Florence and Robert's sister Laura. Together, they enjoyed the most luxurious lifestyle Flint had to offer.

Today, people come from all over for a peek into the Whaley's world. The home has been restored to look as it did when the family lived there. Visitors who come to see the fine furnishings and beautiful architecture are never disappointed, but they are missing the real attraction—GHOSTS!

Over the years, the home has earned quite a reputation as a haunted building. It's easy to see why. Here is an example of the strange things that happen in the mansion. Visitors have reported seeing shadows flicker in the corner of their eyes. When they turn their heads to see what moved—nothing and no one is there! And that's just for starters.

The house is filled with mysterious sounds that cannot be explained. The tinkling of bells can be heard throughout the house, but there are no bells. People also describe hearing the strange sound of rustling coming from empty rooms. Perhaps it is the sound of a long, full Victorian skirt with a crackling crinoline beneath it, the kind that was so popular when the Whaleys first moved into the mansion. If so, I wonder which of the Whaley women—dressed in her finest gown—drifts unseen through the home.

As in most haunted houses, disembodied footsteps can be heard here throughout the building. This sure is scary to those who think they are alone in the building—especially when they are working late at night!

People who are sensitive to the paranormal feel a strong female presence as the footsteps echo through the house. Some have described not being able to catch their breath while in the home. Their breathing returns to normal once they leave the property.

All of this would be enough to convince most people that there's something supernatural in the Whaley House. Motor City Ghost Hunters investigated the home, and they believe it is haunted by multiple members of the Whaley family. They captured otherworldly voices on their digital recorders and found strong fluctuations in their EMF readings. (EMF is short for electromagnetic field.) Many ghost hunters believe that when a spirit is present, it can be detected by a surge of energy. EMF meters can detect the energy that humans cannot sense.

The Whaley House basement is a hotbed of paranormal happenings. Cold spots and strong electromagnetic fields have been detected in the underground rooms. People brave enough to venture into the basement describe the unnerving feeling of being watched. A former director of the museum shared a story about a time when he was in the basement by himself. Without warning, a female voice shrieked directly behind him. Filled with terror, he ran up the stairs without looking back to see where the scream came from. When he mustered up the courage to go back and investigate, the basement was empty, except for him and his pounding heart.

Believe it or not, the basement might not be the spookiest part of the house. There is a great deal of activity in what is known as the Children's Room on the second floor. Curtains move inside the room, even when the windows are closed and there isn't a draft. An old wooden rocking chair rocks on its own, as if it's occupied by an unseen child. The toys in the room get plenty of use from this specter. Rolling toys are often found in the hallway outside the room. It seems as if whoever remains in that room wants to be noticed.

While all of this is certainly creepy, there is no real reason to be afraid of the Whaley House or the spirits who linger in the mansion. The employees of the museum assure visitors that the ghosts here are friendly and no one has ever been harmed by anything paranormal in the building.

Next time you get the chance to check out the Whaley House Museum, stay alert! You never know what you'll see or hear, but it just might be the start of a fantastically spooky adventure!

CHAPTER 3

You Will Not Follow Me Home

Have you ever been ghost hunting? Hunting supernatural beings can be risky business, especially if you are in a genuinely haunted building. If it's ghosts you seek, there might be no better place in Flint to find them than at the Stockton House at Spring Grove.

Why is this house so haunted? Well, for starters, people have died in the building—lots of them! The house saw its first death in 1890 when Thomas Stockton, the original owner of the home, died inside its walls. Eight years later, Thomas's wife Maria, died there, too. As she struggled to take her final breaths, a powerful thunderstorm raged outside. Rain pounded on windows panes. Heavy winds swirled around the home. As Maria drifted into the otherworld, the house was struck by lightning! The sharp crack of electricity pierced the attic. It started a fire! Today, you can still see the charred rafters in the attic from that strange night.

The deaths of the Stocktons may have been the start of the paranormal activity in the house, but deaths in the elegant home continued. In 1920, the building became St. Joseph Hospital. Inside, there were fifty-two beds for sick patients. There was a chapel on the second floor of the house. The nuns who tended to the patients lived in the attic. Did I mention there was a morgue on the first floor? Now, that's spooky!

The house was a hospital for sixteen years. In that time, countless sick people died and crossed over to the other side. The Stockton House saw even more death when it served as a nursing home from 1936 to 1996. With all of those lives coming to an end on the property, there are bound to be a few spirits who choose to stick around.

Lots of ghost hunts have turned up evidence of paranormal activity in the

Stockton House. The hunters use modern equipment to help them detect the presence of spirits. Electromagnetic field meters (EMF) are among the devices used in ghost hunting. When the meters are used in the Stockton House, they ALWAYS light up. Just what—or more importantly, WHO—are these meters detecting?

Modern ghost hunters also use EVP recorders. EVP stands for electronic voice phenomena. These tools can record sounds not detected by human ears. Inside the Stockton House, these recorders have captured the sounds of whistling, whispered voices, and unaccounted-for footsteps. Steve Wood of the Michigan Quest Paranormal Team explored the house in 2017. When interviewed about the spooky mansion, he said it was "one of the most active places we've been to."

The house has so much paranormal activity that you don't need fancy equipment to find it. The unexplained creaking floorboards are familiar to those who spend time in the Stockton House. People often report hearing footsteps in the home when they are alone in the building. Some people think these are the sounds of the Stockton family, still enjoying their beautiful home in the afterlife. Others think it's the sounds of ghostly nurses, still tending to their patients from beyond the grave. The unseen presence walking through the empty house seems very comfortable there.

If you visit the Stockton House in hopes of catching a glimpse of a spine-tingling specter, you might be in luck. Several people have reported spotting a ghostly young boy. His name is thought to be Jonathan. The boy has been seen by ghost hunters and sensed by mediums. Some claim he is looking for his toy train. If you see him, maybe you can help him find it!

Jacqui Richardson works at the Stockton House. She believes the house is haunted with friendly ghosts. When she leads ghost tours and other spooky events in the house, she offers her guests a bit of advice. She tells them that before they leave the home, they must tell the ghosts that dwell inside the home, "You will not follow me home." If you go there in search of ghosts and things get a bit too creepy for comfort, just keep repeating, "You will not follow me home. You will not follow me home." That should work—right?

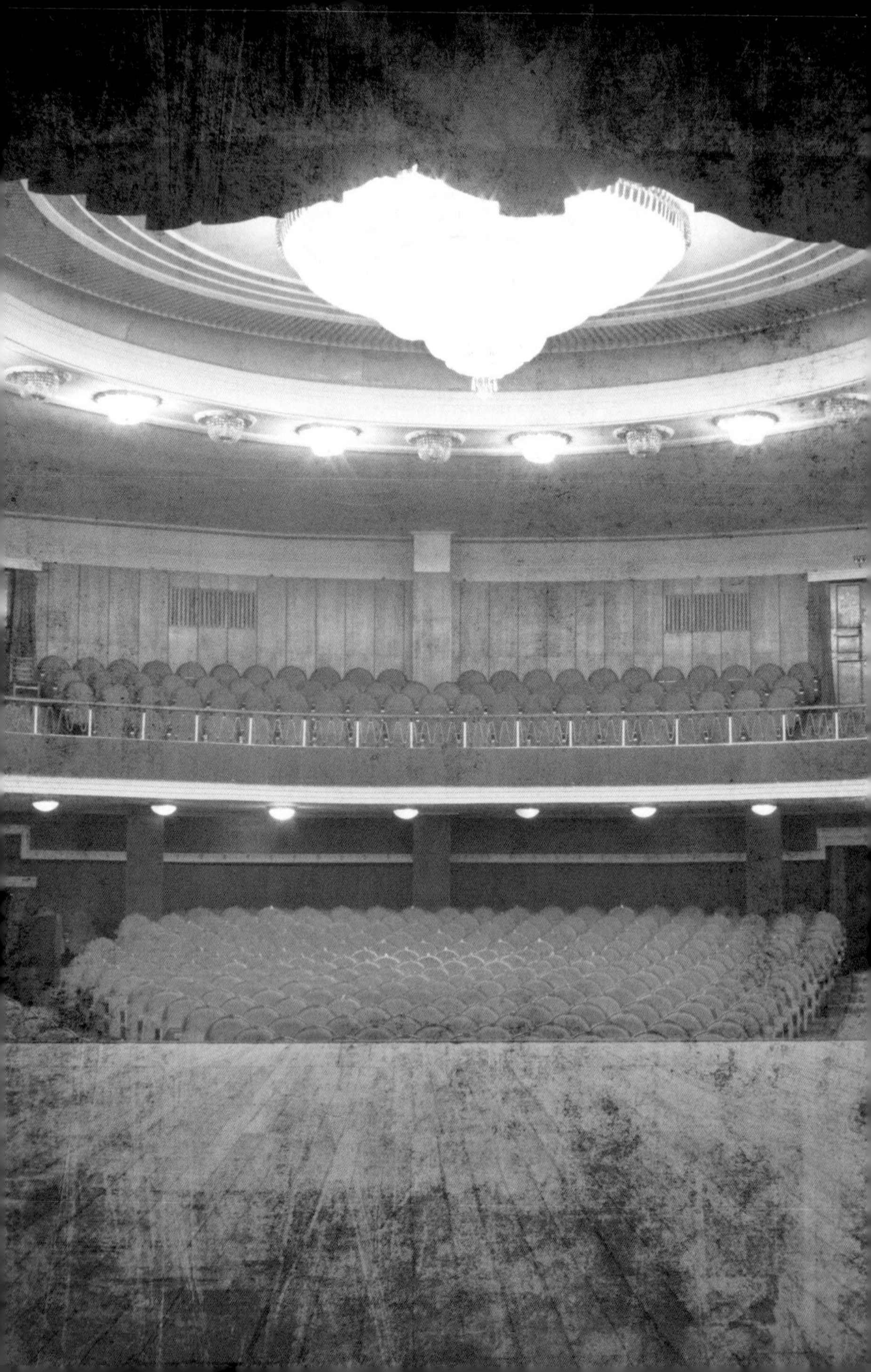

CHAPTER 4

Haunted Happenings at the Capitol Theatre

Imagine this: it is the 1930s. You and your friends are sitting in the Capitol Theatre. Most of the 2,000 seats in the theater are filled with moviegoers, who, just like you, are excited to be in the largest, most lavish theater in Flint. You munch on popcorn in the dark while watching the images flicker across the movie screen. You squirreled away your pennies all week to be able to sit in the deep velvet seat and see the latest film from Hollywood. You are having a wonderful time!

You and your friends are on the edges of your seats watching a gunfight on the screen. The speakers in the theater are so loud, it sounds like guns are being fired right in the theater! You and your friends cheer when the good guys win, and the movie soon comes to an end.

When the lights come back on, you hear someone scream. You squint to see what people are pointing at, and then you spot it. An usher is slumped upon the ground near the rear exit of the theater in a pool of blood. He is dead!

This shocking event really happened in the Capitol Theatre during the 1930s! Gunshots were fired during a robbery in the alley behind the theater. One of the stray bullets shot through the back door of the theater, striking the usher. No one heard the shot or the man's cries for help over the sounds of the movie. It was only after the movie ended that people in the Capitol Theatre discovered a man died just feet away as they watched their movie.

Could this unexpected murder be the reason the Capitol Theatre is haunted? That wouldn't be surprising. But if you consider all of the eerie happenings that occur inside the theater, you might conclude there may be more than one spirit who calls the landmark theater home.

The Capitol Theatre has a long history. It was a luxurious movie house when it opened in 1928. In 1957, the theater was modernized and expanded. The theater started hosting live music performances in the 1970s and still does today. As time passed, the theater fell into disrepair. But there were people who loved the theater too much to let it be torn down. Together, they figured out a way to save the theater. After lots of remodeling, the Capitol was returned to its former glory. It reopened to entertain new generations of Michiganders in 2017.

Could it be the construction in the building that keeps the lingering spirits restless? Paranormal activity has been reported from the basement to the balcony of the theater and everywhere in between. Shadowy specters have been spotted on the stage, at the back door, and in the balcony.

Spine-tingling screams and moans have been heard throughout the building. The sound of singing from an unseen songstress sometimes joins the chorus of unearthly sounds in the old theater. Perhaps most terrifying are the sounds of tapping (sometimes even knocking) accompanied by shrieks that seem to be coming from INSIDE the walls! No one knows who or what is responsible for the bone-chilling sounds!

As you could probably guess, the apparition of an usher haunts the theater—but he is not alone. People have also spotted a figure described as a workman in the basement of the building. A lucky few have witnessed the ghostly, glowing figure of a young girl on the stage. Who she is and why she is tied to the theater remains a mystery.

The Capitol Theatre is beautiful, old, and definitely haunted. The next time you are in the theater, take a look around you. If you see a man who looks a little hazy walking in the aisles, take a closer look. You may have just spotted the usher who was gunned down in the theater so many years ago. If you do, I just hope the spot next to you isn't open. And if it is, I hope he doesn't feel like having a seat...

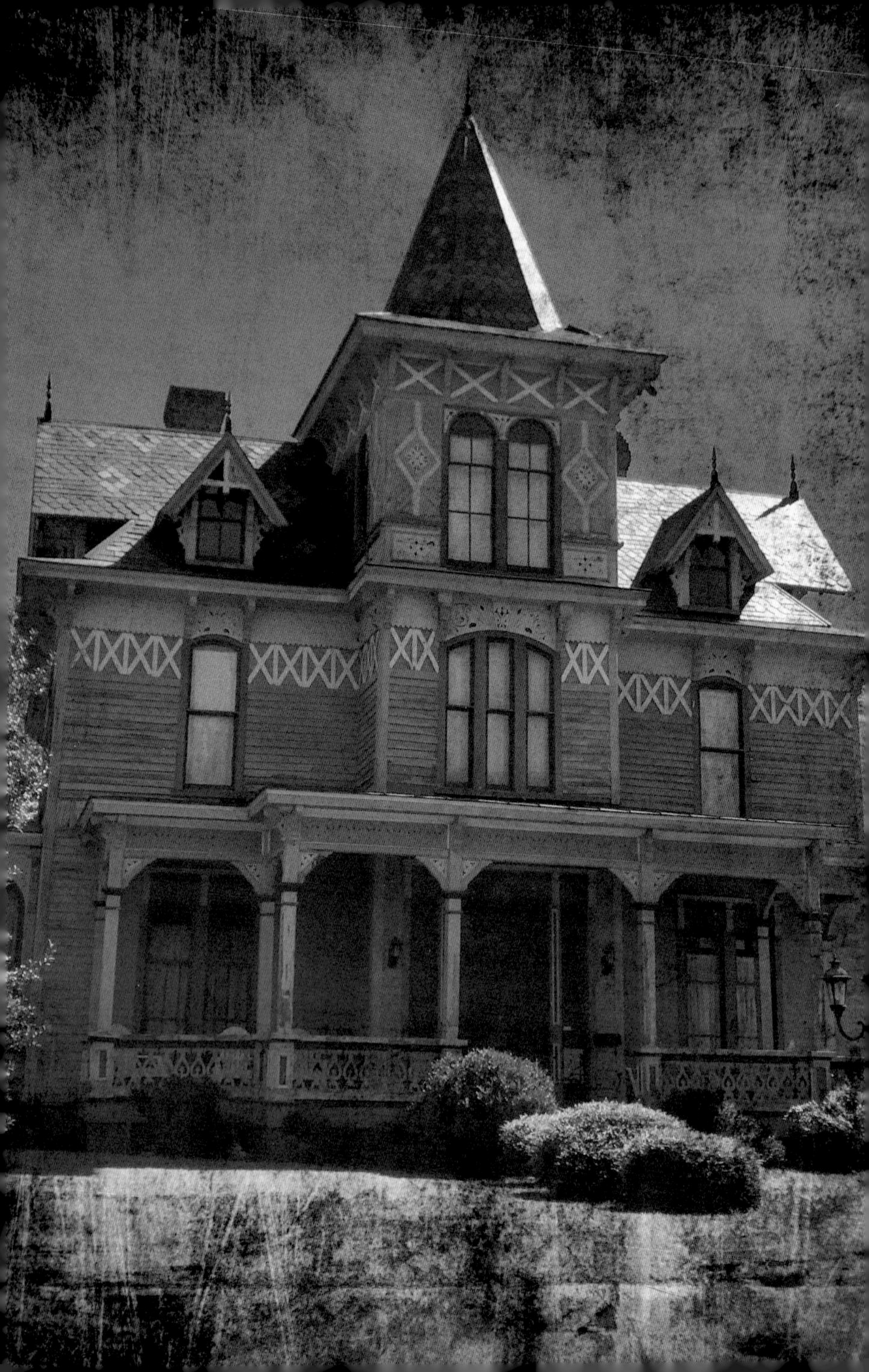

CHAPTER 5

(Very) Creepy Carriage Town

Everyone has heard of a haunted house, but how about a haunted NEIGHBORHOOD? It seems unlikely, yet the historic neighborhood of Carriage Town has some of Flint's oldest homes and, if you believe the stories, more ghosts per block than any other neighborhood in the city!

Here are just a few of the homes that make this neighborhood spook-tacular.

The old Traxler House on Mason Street is said to have an otherworldly resident. The house was once owned by David Traxler, best remembered as the co-owner of the Flint Pantaloon Company, which, in 1896, started making "the best four-dollar pants in the world." Even though the Traxler family left the home long ago, something important might have been left behind. People have seen a woman in a second-floor window of the home. That wouldn't be a big deal, but that woman definitely does not live in the house. She has been spotted for years, and it doesn't look like she is going to move on anytime soon.

If you think that sounds creepy, wait until you hear what happens in the house right across the street. There is an unseen entity in the house. Lots of people have ghosts in their houses, so it should be a manageable problem, but not with this ghost. This spirit TOUCHES them! The people who live in the house report that they can feel invisible hands trying to push them down the staircase of the home. Yikes! I'd be packing my bags and looking for a new place to live faster than you can say "haunted Halloween hideaway." How about you?

Moving on from Mason Street, there are some interesting happenings on Begole Street in the former house of Joseph and Mary Ann Dunbar. The couple lived in the house until they died. Mary Ann passed away in 1913, and Joseph died inside the house in 1914. It seems the couple might have been awfully attached to the house because it appears that they are still there. The bedroom the Dunbars shared is so spooky that the kids who live in the house now won't go into the room. Why? Because they can SEE someone in there!

Saving the best for last, let's talk about the Paine House on Fourth Avenue. It was built in

1907 for David and Lilla Paine. Lilla really loved her house. After her husband died in 1918, however, she struggled to afford it. Rather than move, she came up with an idea to make more money. She modified the home so she could rent out part of it to tenants. Lilla was able to live in her home until 1932, when she went to live with her sister. That should be the end of the story, but it is not.

The people who own Lilla's home today are CERTAIN it is haunted. They hear the footsteps of an unseen walker. It is common for them to hear unexplained crashing sounds in the house. Sometimes pictures that have been firmly secured to the wall fall to the ground for no reason. The people who live there now even report being touched by an unseen hand!

They have done everything they can to release the spirit from the Paine house. They have had it blessed, but that didn't work. They have had it smudged, but that didn't work. The owners of the house aren't sure what to do next. It looks like they are going to have to get used to having a noisy, invisible roommate who doesn't like their taste in wall decorations.

After hearing those stories, it sure seems like Carriage Town is a haunted neighborhood. Think about it—these are just the tales about the haunted houses we KNOW about in the Carriage Town. Can you imagine what else is lurking there that has yet to be told? A spine-tingling thought!

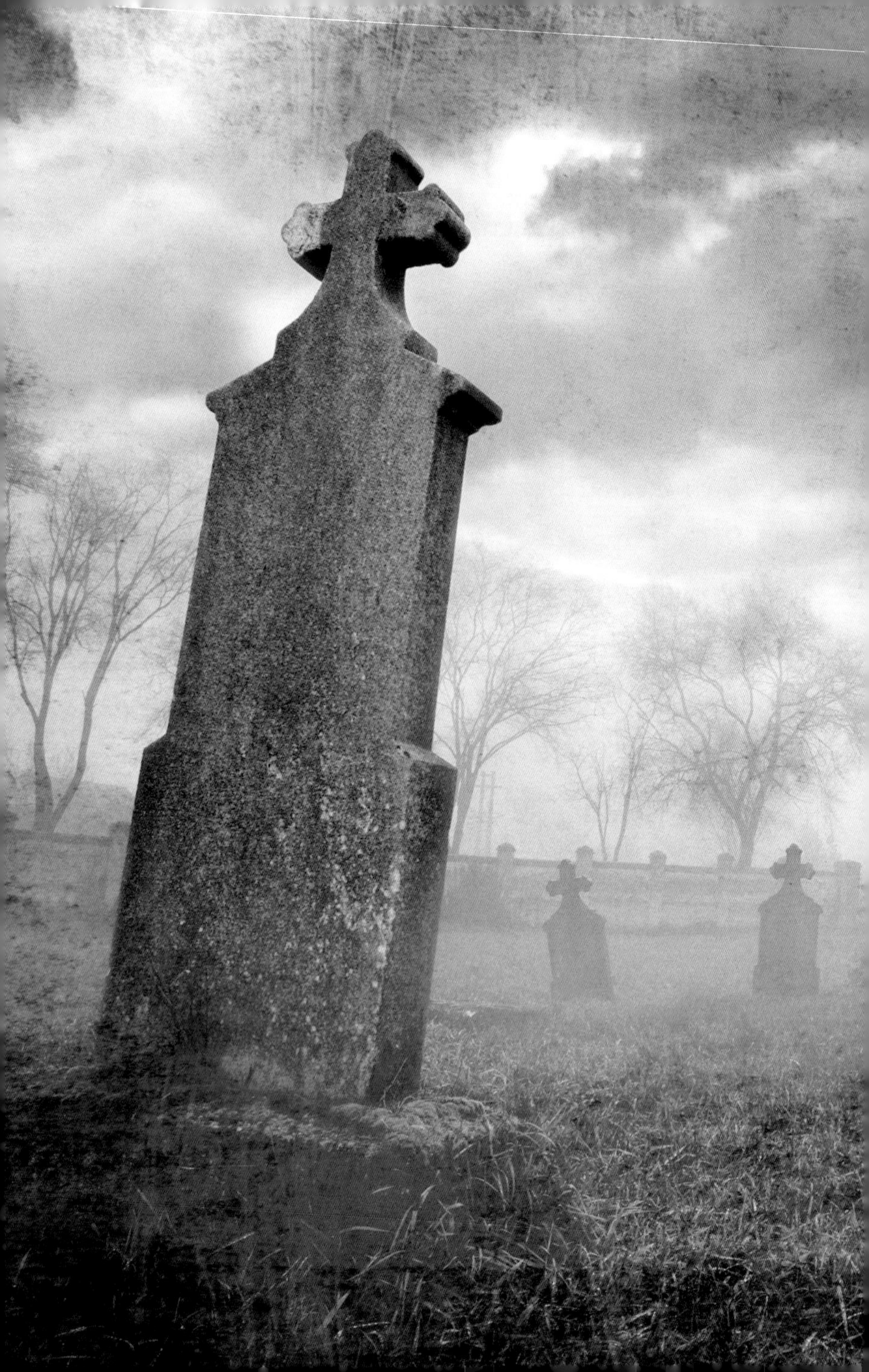

CHAPTER 6

Ghosts in the Graveyard

Have you ever played the game "Ghost in the Graveyard?" It's a spooky nighttime game for three or more people that combines tag and hide-and-go-seek.

In this game, you choose one player to be "it." That player is the "ghost." The ghost hides while everyone else closes their eyes and counts "one o'clock, two o'clock, three o'clock" until they get to midnight. When the group yells "MIDNIGHT," they run in search of the ghost. When players spot the ghost, they shout, "Ghost in the graveyard! Run, run, run!" Then all players attempt to get safely home before the ghost catches them. The ghost begins to chase the players. If the ghost tags someone, that person becomes a ghost in the next round.

Sounds fun, right? Visiting these Flint graveyards is a bit like playing that game. Except the ghosts in these stories aren't hiding. Do you dare to seek them out?

Flint has many graveyards, but none of them seems to have as many spooky stories connected to them as Sunset Hills Cemetery. People find the life-like statues in the cemetery more than just creepy. They are outright scared of them! You've probably heard the tales of these statues watching you as you pass by them. Or that the statues come to life at night. It's all spooky stuff, but no story tops the legend of the "Crack the Whip" statue.

This bronze statue depicts eight life-sized kids holding hands while playing Crack the Whip. Stories have swirled around the statue since it was placed in the cemetery in the 1980s. Those who visit it claim they can hear children laughing and playing as they walk closer to the work of art. Others believe they hear the sounds of a child sobbing when they look at the happy faces on the realistic sculpture.

One of the girls depicted in the statue has lost her shoe. The bronze shoe appears a few yards from the statue of the children. Visitors often slip their feet into the shoe to see if it fits. This is like playing Cinderella, but instead of good things happening when the shoe fits, the outcome is bad. Very bad. Some say if the shoe fits your foot, something terrible will happen to you. Others say it means you will die soon. Most terrifying, they say if you try the shoe at exactly midnight and it fits, the statue of the children will come to life. But that can't really be true. Right? Or can it?

The Glenwood Cemetery is just a few miles from the Sunset Hills Cemetery. People call it Flint's historic cemetery because so many well-known people from Flint's past are buried here. If you are walking down a street that is named after someone, chances are that person can be found inside the gates of the Glenwood Cemetery.

It was built to be a beautiful and tranquil spot to get away from the heat and noise of the city. It was also a great place for people to secretly meet. After all, graveyards are often pretty empty. Well, at least empty of living people! In 1931, Leslie Casteel and his girlfriend, Helen, drove out to Glenwood Cemetery for a private conversation.

Things didn't go well inside the car, and before long, Leslie had three bullets in his body. Helen then dragged his lifeless body out of the car and drove off. She would later explain that Leslie forced her to drive to the cemetery. She then said that the pair fought, and he pulled a gun on her. Helen went on to say she wrestled the gun away from Leslie and shot him in self-defense. It was quite a story!

At first, people believed Helen. Leslie didn't have much money or education, and he had been in trouble with the law before. People were willing to believe he was up to no good. Helen, on the other hand, was a rich, young girl from a well-known family. But as the police began to look into the case, Helen's story fell apart. In the end, Helen was convicted of second-degree murder, and Leslie Casteel became a ghost. What? Did you think this story wouldn't take a scary turn? Yes, many believe the spirit of Leslie remains in the spot in the cemetery where he took his last breath. Would you like to take a stroll through Glenwood Cemetery to see if you can spot him?

Sloan Museum

CHAPTER 7

Spooky Sightings at the Sloan Museum

Do you think you'd know a ghost if you saw one? The answer might not be as obvious as you think! At least it wasn't for a man who worked at the Sloan Museum.

Joshua and his coworker Jen were working at the museum together one afternoon. As closing time approached, Joshua let visitors know that the museum would soon lock its doors for the day. He talked to a group of four adults and a woman with two children. Both groups let him know they'd be leaving soon.

After Joshua did his final walk through the museum, he went to the front desk. He was busy with his closing duties as he waited for the last two groups to leave the building. Soon, a group approached the exit, and Joshua waved goodbye to the four adults. Now he only had to wait for the woman with the two children to leave so he and Jen could lock up the museum for the night.

Impatient to leave for the day, Joshua decided to find the group and escort them to the exit. He went to the place where had last seen them, the children's area. It was empty. He searched room after room, but he could not find the group. There is only one exit in the museum. How could they have left without being seen?

Meanwhile, Jen's mom was waiting for her outside the museum. Jen sent her mom a text to let her know she was running late. She and Joshua still needed to find the woman and the two children before they closed the museum for the night. Jen asked her mom if she had seen anyone leave the museum. She hoped the missing visitors had somehow slipped by the front desk. Jen's mom replied that she had seen the group of four adults leave, but she had not seen anyone else leave the building.

Determined to find the woman and children, Joshua and Jen searched every corner of the museum, but they could not find a living soul. The group HAD been there. Joshua talked to them. It was impossible for them to disappear into thin air!

In exasperation, Jen reviewed the ticket sales for the day. As she got to the end of the list, a shiver ran up her spine. They did not have a single transaction for one adult and two children. The trio vanished because they had never been there—at least, not in the flesh. Unnerved and more than a little frightened, Joshua and Jen quickly locked up the museum and fled.

That is not the only time spectral visitors have been spotted in the Sloan Museum. The museum was hosting a private party one night. A guest mentioned to Joshua that he really liked that the museum had some costumed staff working at the party. Joshua was puzzled by the man's statement. Joshua and Greg were the only museum employees working that night, and they were both wearing their regular clothing. He asked the guest to describe what he had seen. The man explained that he admired the costume of the woman who was wearing a floor-length gown with a high collar. He went on to describe the cameo she wore around her neck and that her dark brown hair was tied in a bun.

Stunned, Joshua just shook his head. He told the man he and Greg were the only Sloan Museum employees working that night. He then startled the man by explaining that he had welcomed each of the guests to the event that night, and there was not a single person wearing anything like what he had described. Shaken by the realization that he has seen an apparition, the man turned pale and excused himself.

Over 60,000 kids visit the Sloan Museum each year. If you are one of those kids, keep your eyes wide open. Take a closer look at the people you see in the building. Are they slightly blurred? Do their feet touch the ground, or are they gliding through the air? Ghosts might be hiding in plain sight. And one more reminder: if you see a lady wearing a swishy old-fashioned skirt, take a second look! Chances are she does NOT work in the museum and you might have just spotted a ghost!

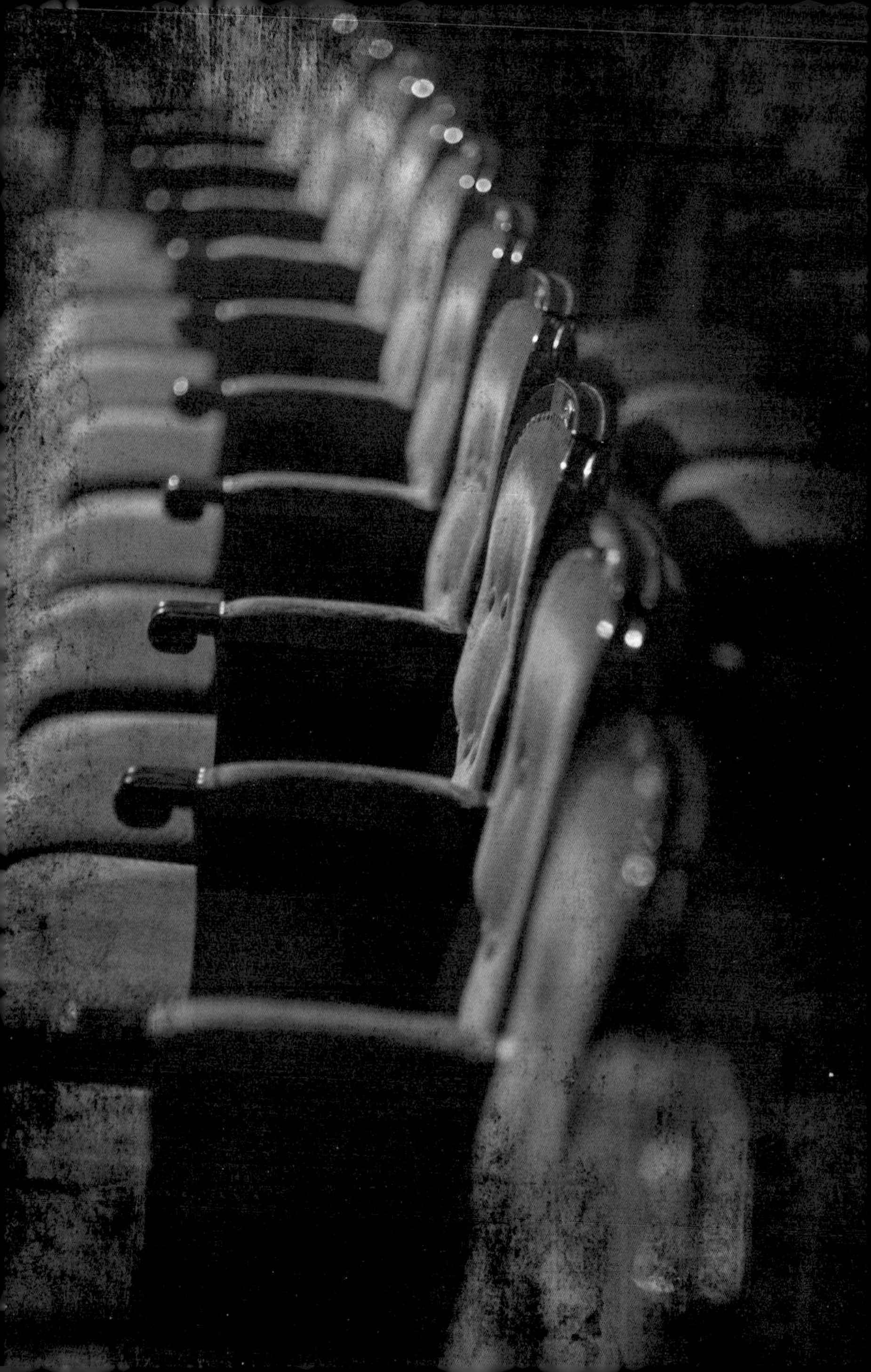

CHAPTER 8

Exit, Stage Left

Theaters are some of the most haunted buildings in the world. It seems every city has a theater still served by a ghostly usher or actors who are still taking their final bows long after they have been buried in their graves. The Whiting guarantees that Flint has a place on the list of cities with a haunted theater.

The Whiting has one strange difference: the ghost that haunts this theater was never part of the show. This spirit did not act on stage. Or take tickets. Or even show guests to their seats. In life, this person operated behind the scenes. But in the afterlife, he has decided to take center stage.

In one story I heard, a member of the staff was cleaning up after a show late at night. He glanced at the stage and saw a man in work clothes standing on the stage. He was startled because he thought he was the only one in the theater. When he looked back at the man to ask who he was, the man had vanished! He searched backstage for the mysterious man, but there wasn't a trace of him. The staff member decided the Whiting was clean enough for one night and promptly left the building, saving the rest of his duties until the next day, when there would be others in the theater.

That was not the last time this mysterious man was seen. In 2009, the Mid-Michigan

Paranormal Investigators came to the theater to investigate the claims that the Whiting was haunted. The team used modern ghost detecting tools, like EVP recorders and EMF meters. Remember, these tools can detect things in a room that cannot be seen or heard by humans. They searched the building, noting that their EMF meters displayed strange fluctuations throughout the building that could not be explained. Their audio recorders picked up music that could not be heard by human ears and the distant murmur of voices, despite the fact that the investigators remained silent while recording. But the thing that chilled them the most was the apparition seen by a team member.

The apparition appeared in shadow, but the investigator described him as wearing heavy boots and work clothes. He sounded just like the specter the cleaner had described seeing on stage! Chances are the apparition who appears on stage is an unfortunate construction worker who lived many years ago and was involved in a tragic accident. While working, he fell from a scaffolding and landed on the stage with a sickening thud. People rushed to his aid, but his injuries were too great for him to recover. He died upon the stage—the same stage where people report seeing the ghostly image of a man in work clothes. Coincidence?

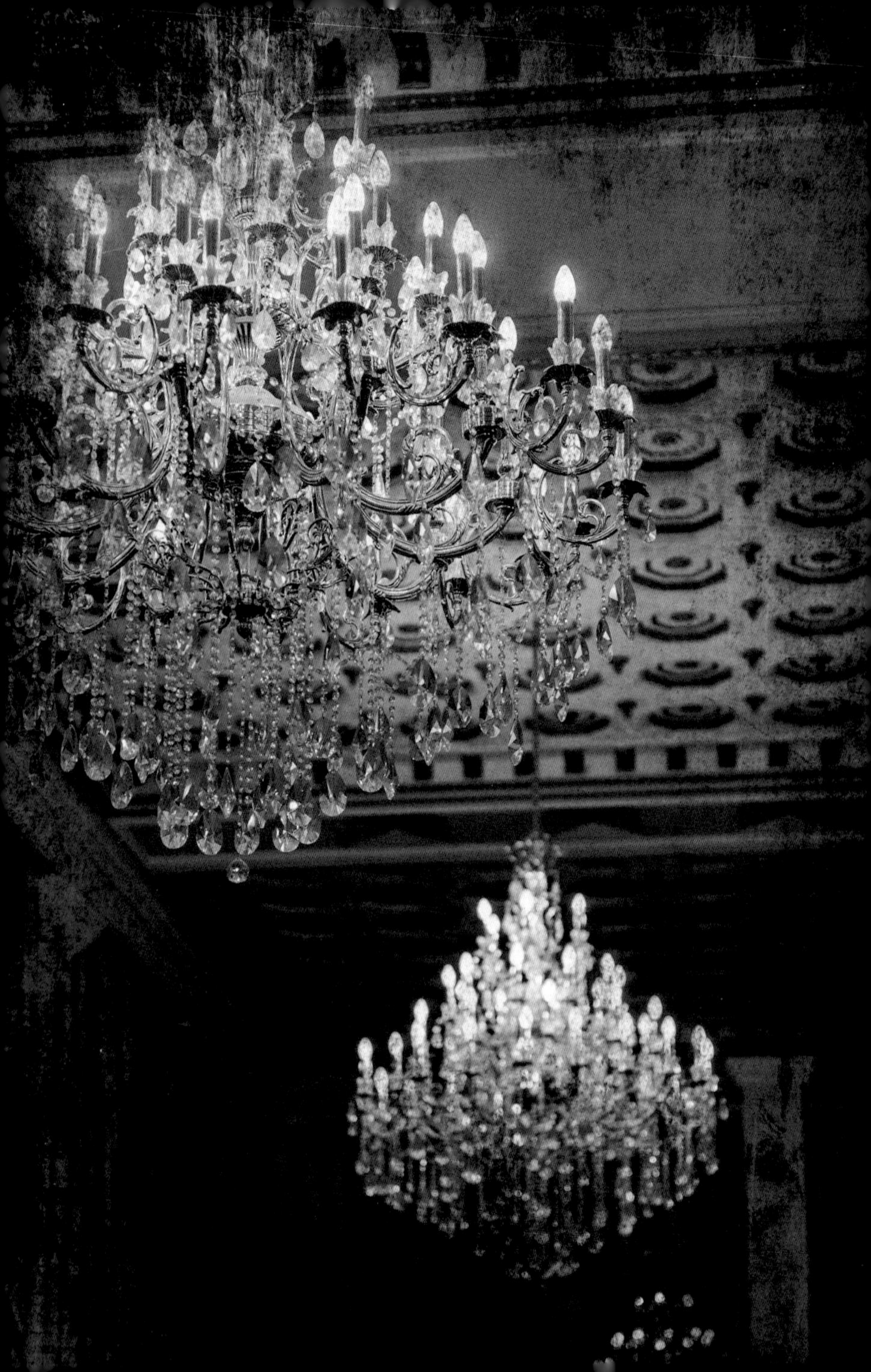

CHAPTER 9

Check Out Time: NEVER

When the Durant Hotel opened its doors in 1920, it was the finest hotel in Flint. Wealthy businessmen, celebrities, and visitors who loved luxury flocked to the popular hotel. On the first floor, there were elegant shops that sold jewelry, furs, and other extravagant items. Night after night, the ballrooms were filled with well-dressed couples twirling around the dance floors. Every notable person who passed through Flint spent time in the downtown hot spot.

The hotel was named for its biggest investor, the president and founder of General Motors, William C. Durant. An eight-room hotel suite was built in his honor on the hotel's sixth floor. Durant often visited the hotel until his death in 1947. His habit of hanging around the hotel during his lifetime seems to have continued into his afterlife.

Many believe Durant's spirit still lingers in the hotel. Rumors that he haunted the hotel began in the 1960s. Around that time, visitors started seeing the spectral figure of a man roaming the sixth floor. The unmistakable sounds of footsteps were heard coming from the vacant rooms of his former luxury suite. Music and laughter from celebrations hosted long ago spill out of empty ballrooms. The spirits continued the party that had ended long ago.

Over the years, the hotel stopped drawing crowds. After years of struggling to stay open, it closed in 1973. But an unknown number of spirits continue to enjoy the hospitality of the former Durant Hotel.

People could no longer experience the specter of Durant on the sixth floor or hear the sounds of otherworldly parties. But the spirits in the hotel found another way to make themselves known. Periodically, the Motor Hotel sign on top of the abandoned building would turn itself on. The red lights on the sign lit up the night sky. The glowing light reminded the people of Flint that the building might not be as vacant as they thought.

Not all of the spirits that linger in the Durant Hotel are reliving happy events.

One of the best-known ghosts associated with the landmark building is Lawrence Hutchins.

Lawrence's sad story begins on October 10, 1928. After a long day, he was walking home. As he passed the Durant Hotel, he heard someone call for help. Lawrence ran toward the sound and found Anne, a waitress at the coffee shop next to the hotel. She was being bullied by two brothers, Sammy and Melvin. The brothers cornered Anne and would not let her move past them.

Lawrence moved in to help Anne, and he was punched by Sammy. When the fight started, Anne ran away. She looked back and saw Melvin slug Lawrence in the jaw. When the brothers stopped pummeling Lawrence, he staggered away down the street. Bruised and bloody, Lawrence did not walk far before he collapsed onto the sidewalk. Seeing the man who just helped her was in need of help himself, Anne ran over to offer aid. Lawrence was sprawled on the sidewalk in front of the hotel. While Lawrence's blood seeped into

the pavement, he and Anne waited for an ambulance to arrive.

Lawrence was dead before help appeared. Anne watched as his broken body was loaded into the ambulance and taken to the morgue. But that was not the last time the man was seen on that street.

There are those who claim to have seen the apparition of Lawrence strolling down the sidewalk in front of the building. Could it be that Lawrence's sudden and unexpected death left his spirit unsettled? Maybe his exit from the earthly realm was so swift that his spirit does not know his body is dead? Or perhaps Lawrence believed himself to be too young to die, so his spirit continues to restlessly roam among the living?

Today, the building that was once Flint's most luxurious hotel is known as the Durant. Instead of ballrooms and suites for millionaires, the building now contains condominiums and businesses. New people have moved in, but the spirit of the hotel remains. The ghostly bands still play in the ballrooms that have been boarded up for decades. Diamonds worn by partygoers continue to sparkle in the light of chandeliers that haven't been lit since 1973. For the ghosts that still remain in the building, the party has never stopped.

CHAPTER 10

The Macabre Masonic Temple

Did you know that Flint has a Masonic Temple? You might have heard people talk about Freemasonry. The members of this men's club are called Masons. Some people think the organization is nothing more than a social group for men. Others think it is a mysterious secret organization with dangerous secrets. There are Masons all over the world. Some very famous people were Masons, including

George Washington, Benjamin Franklin, pioneer Davy Crockett, astronaut Buzz Aldrin, and even King Edward VII of England, just to name a few!

Some of Flint's most best-known former citizens were Masons, including Walter Chrysler and James Whiting. The group met at the Flint Masonic Temple, which was built in 1911. The location was a popular spot for members to gather and socialize. For many Masons, the temple was their favorite place to be. Some of them liked it so much, not even death could stop them from visiting!

It has been many years since the building served its original purpose. It is no longer connected to any organizations of Masons. Modern visitors come to the building to attend special events such as weddings and to see live entertainment. Even though the building is no longer linked to Masons, that hasn't stopped the spirits of former members from lingering in the temple.

If you want to hear from spooky tales of the haunted temple, Ted Valley has some strange stories for you. For years, Ted had an office in the building. He is a skeptic when it comes to ghosts, but he has had some experiences that just might make YOU a believer!

Ted was working alone in the building late one night. It was well after midnight when he heard a strange rattling sound. He paused and listened carefully. When he heard the sound again, he knew it was coming from the locker room. It was the sound of old metal lockers opening and closing. He was confused, as he was the only one in the temple. Besides, no one would have any interest in getting into the lockers; they had not been used in years. There was nothing inside of them except for the belongings of some long dead Masons.

It suddenly occurred to him who *would* want to get into the locker room: ghosts of those long-dead Masons! He shouted into the dark hallway, "Knock it off! I'm busy working here." It was silent in the empty building for a few moments. Just as Ted relaxed and began working again, he heard a loud bang. It was the unmistakable sound of a locker door slamming!

Feeling brave, Ted called out, "Listen, I told you I am working here! The more you screw around, the longer I'll be here." Then everything was silent—for a few moments, at least. After several quiet minutes, Ted heard a sound. Footsteps! Someone was walking on the floor above him. The unseen spirit paced back and forth across the room until Ted left the building. It certainly seemed as if the spirits were eager for Ted to leave.

That was not the only time Ted experienced strange things in the Flint temple. While he was helping to produce a play in the building's theater, another unexplainable event occurred—and this time, there were plenty of witnesses. A group was working on a play about the ghosts that appear in that famous Christmas story featuring Scrooge and Tiny Tim. In that story—*A Christmas Carol* by Charles Dickens—ghosts come back from the dead to warn Scrooge that if he doesn't change his ways, he'll be tortured in the afterlife, just like they are. An actor was rehearsing a speech delivered by one of the ghosts who haunt Scrooge on stage.

Suddenly, a lightbulb fell out of its socket and crashed onto the actor's head! Moments before, it had been firmly screwed into the light fixture and glowing. How did the lightbulb become unscrewed from the light socket? Were the spirits who make the Masonic Temple their home in the afterlife trying to send their own warnings from beyond the grave?

Ted isn't the only person who has had spooky experiences at the Flint Masonic Temple. People who have visited the temple have reported all kinds of eerie happenings throughout the building. Guests have seen shadowy figures flickering across the walls in seemingly empty rooms. Faint sounds of organ music drift down vacant hallways, yet no earthly hands touch the instrument's keys!

The York floor seems to be the most active spot in a building filled with supernatural happenings. One night while preparing for an event there, workers got the shock of their lives. A faint movement in the doorway got their attention. They turned to look and gasped! In front of their eyes was the figure of a woman in white. The translucent spirit hovered along the wall. As suddenly as she appeared, the lady in white drifted away. Her identity remains unknown. But she will never be forgotten by those who saw her.

With so many eerie events occurring throughout the building, the chances of having a paranormal experience while in the Flint Masonic Temple seem pretty high. If you are brave enough to enter its doors, pay careful attention to everything you see and hear. Notice the shadows that move in the corner of your eye. Strain to listen for sounds that come from vacant rooms. And if you feel a chill running up your spine, it might be more than just fear. You may not be alone, even if it looks like you are.

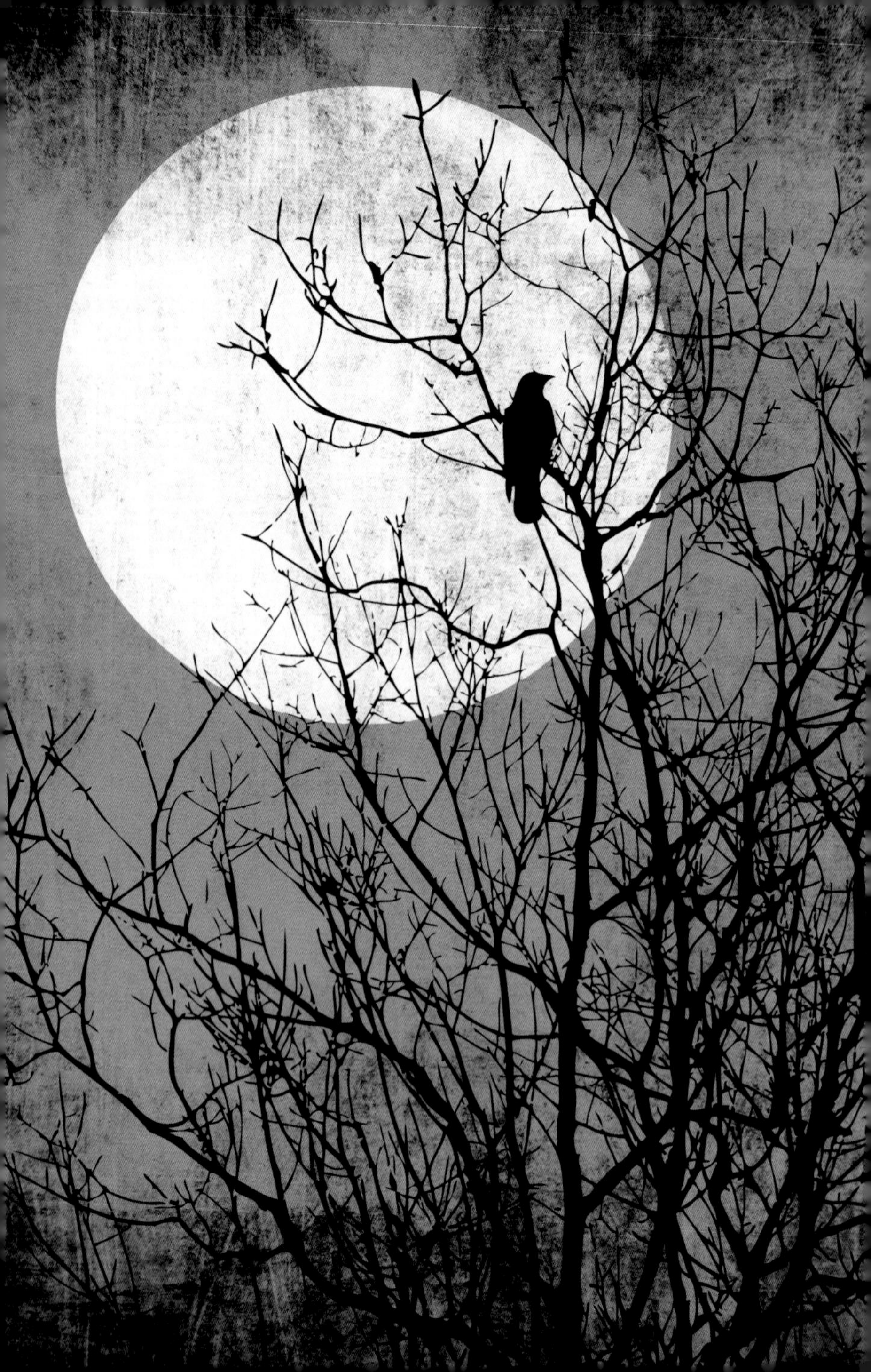

CHAPTER 11

William, Is That You?

It may be just a rumor, but I heard a very creepy story about a woman who had just gotten a job at the historic redbrick Dryden Building. I didn't catch her name, but let's say it was Julia. She loved working there. It was her first time working late. She had heard rumors the building was haunted, but she didn't believe a word of it. Sure, she started to feel a bit uneasy after all of her coworkers left for the day. But that was probably just because she was not used to the creaks and groans of the old building. "Anyway," she thought, "ghosts aren't real, so there is nothing to worry about."

Hours passed as she continued to work. She looked out the window and saw the light of the full moon shining down on the empty street below. It was so late, she was certain she was the only person left in the building. She had just a few more things to finish, and then she could go home.

Rising from her chair, Julia walked out of her office and into the hallway to grab some paperwork. Her footsteps echoed in the empty hallway. She noticed her shadow looming as she continued walking. Suddenly, she froze. What was that sound she just heard? She held her breath and listened. She heard footsteps on the stairs. She felt a shiver of fear run up her spine.

She shook head and laughed nervously to herself. "There is nothing to be afraid of," Julia reassured herself. "It is probably just someone else who is also working late." But just to be on the safe side, she quickened her pace. As soon as Julia started walking faster, those footsteps behind her sped up as well. Before long, she was running. She could hear the footsteps getting closer and closer to her. Who was chasing her?

She reached the end of the corridor. There was nowhere left to run. In an instant, Julia decided to confront the person following her. Clenching her hands into fists, she spun on her heels. Ready for a fight, turned around. She saw...nothing. The dark hallway was empty. The footsteps that she was certain were right behind her were gone. She was all alone. The only sound she could hear was her heart pounding with fear.

Confused and shaken, she decided to head home immediately. She didn't understand what happened in the hallway, but she knew she had to get out of there. Fast!

She rushed to the exit and took a big gulp of night air. She started to relax. Julia knew she hadn't imagined it. Someone or something had chased her down the hallway and then disappeared. But how? Relieved to be safely out of the Dryden Building, she headed home.

The next morning, Julia told her new coworkers about her late-night experience in the Dryden Building. She described being chased, only to turn around and find herself all alone in an empty hallway. She knew it sounded crazy, but it really happened! She needed an explanation.

Instead of being surprised by her story, her coworker Noah just laughed. "You were on the third floor, right?"

Julia nodded her head in agreement. "How did you know?" she asked.

"Oh, we should have warned you! That is where old Mr. Paterson hangs out," Noah said with a grin.

Confused, Julia asked, "Mr. Paterson? Is he the night watchman?"

"Oh no, "chuckled Noah. "You know, Mr. Paterson. William A. Paterson! The man who built this building and named it after his wife."

"I don't get it, Noah. This building was built in 1902. There is no way this Paterson guy is still around. Even if he is, he would be too old to run after me like he did last night."

Noah shrugged his shoulders. "Well, you are half right. Paterson died in 1921, but he is still hanging around. At least, that is what everyone says."

Emma, who was listening to the conversation added, "If you didn't like being chased, DEFINITELY stay out of the bathroom on the third floor. There is something in there. Something scary. I've never seen it, but when you walk into the room," he paused to shiver. "I don't know what it is, but you can *sense* it.

It feels dark. Sinister. Just take my word for it. Use the bathrooms on any other floor. Just NOT on the third floor."

Julia walked back to her desk, stunned at what she heard from Noah and Emma. She realized if she was going to continue to work at the Dryden Building, she would have to change her mind about ghosts. After her experience, she felt certain that ghosts are real. And even more certain that she was NEVER going to work late in the Dryden Building again!

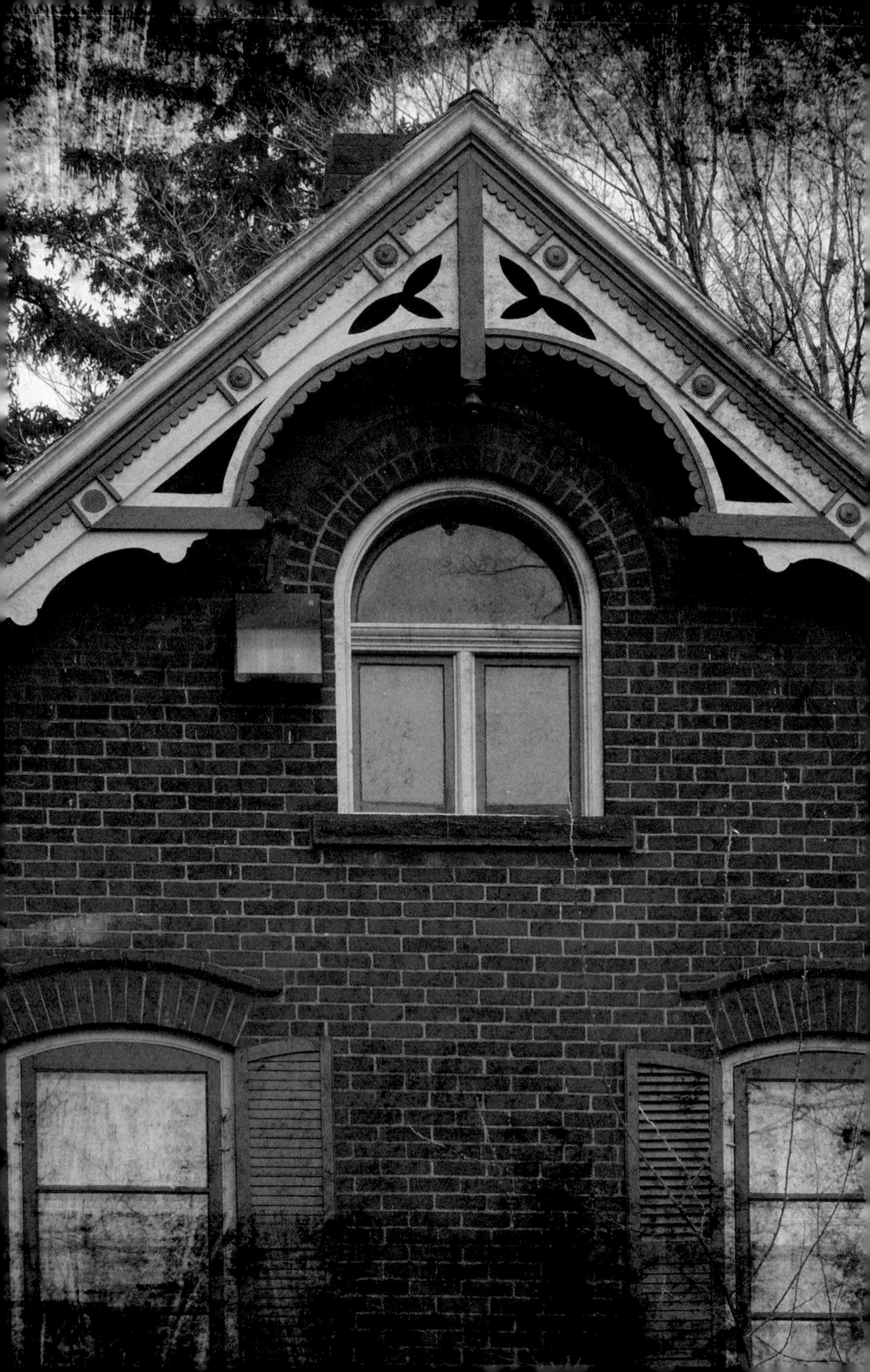

CHAPTER 12

The Home Too Comfortable to Leave

Have you ever loved a place so much that you never wanted to leave it? Jennie Milner Cornwall spent most of her eighty years in a home that is now known as the Cornwall Building. You might have heard the rumors that Jennie's former home is haunted. Could it be that she was so comfortable in the house, she couldn't imagine existing anywhere else?

Why move on to the other side when she was perfectly content inside her cherished home?

Jennie's father was Er Milner. He made his fortune in the lumber business. He bought the home that would become known as the Cornwall Building in 1883, although at the time, it was just the Milner family's home. Er lived in the luxurious home with his wife Lucy and their daughters Jennie and Winnie. Everyone in town admired the house. They were impressed that it was designed by Elijah Meyer. If that name sounds familiar, it is because he is the same man who designed the capitol building in Lansing!

Years passed, and young Jennie met John Cornwall, the man whose name would become forever attached to this building. John was a hardworking man from England. He and his sister created a successful business after they moved to the United States. John and Jennie were both wealthy, young, and single. Love bloomed between the pair. Before long, the couple were engaged to be married.

The duo was married inside the family home in 1885. Members of Flint's high society gathered to celebrate the happy couple. John and Jennie received many fine gifts from their guests, but nothing compared to the gift Jennie's father gave the couple. He gave her the house as a wedding present! Er knew how much Jennie loved the family home, so he signed the deed of the house over to her.

The Milner family remained close after Jennie and John married. Jennie helped tend to her dad as he got older. She took care of him until he died in 1898. Er's death was not the last death that would touch the Cornwall house. John died in the home from kidney disease in 1921. Jennie continued to live in the home she loved until she died inside its walls in 1943. In the end, she spent sixty years of her life in her beloved home.

It seems as if her death did not end Jennie's connection to the building. Those who pass outside of the home at night report seeing people in the windows. The people inside are wearing clothing that was popular more than one hundred years ago. Jennie, wearing a long dress, with her hair swept up in a style from long ago, reveals herself to passersby. But it is clear she is not alone in her mansion. Who are the other figures that have been spotted roaming the home at night?

One of the spirits that joins Jennie in her nighttime walks could be her husband, John. He lived in the home with Jennie for 36 years. Perhaps, like her, he is having a hard time moving on. It might also be her father, Er, who completed the construction on the home and spent many happy years there. Perhaps the family might even welcome visitors from the other side?

It's anyone's guess who the spirits who spend their nights in the Cornwall Building. But it's clear they don't mind being seen. The group seems to be quite comfortable here. I don't think they have plans to move on any time soon. How about you? Is there any place that you've been that you'd like to stay... forever?

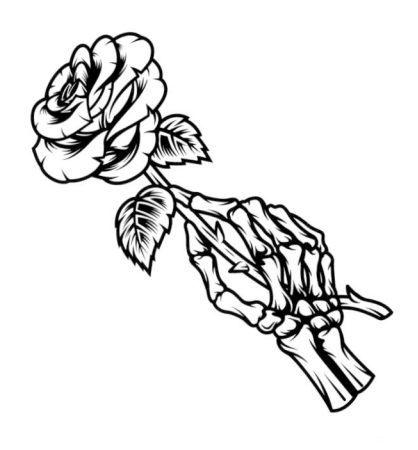

Flint River

CHAPTER 13

A Walk Along the Flint River

People have always flocked to the banks of the Flint River. For generations, the river was the center of city life. Flint citizens drank its water. They bathed in it. They used it for transportation. With all the activity on the river, it is not surprising that more than a few ghosts still linger on its banks, and I heard a story about two boys who had an encounter with them.

One day, brothers (I think their names were Charlie and Henry) were walking along the river. The sun had just started to set, and with each minute that passed, the sky grew darker. The boys had not planned to stay out so late. They had spent the day along the river, skipping stones in the murky waters, looking for frogs, and hunting for treasures that might have washed ashore. They found bits of old mirrors, shards of smashed porcelain that had probably once been fancy dishes, and plenty of garbage but no real treasures.

The crickets were chirping as they headed home. The brothers were muddy from their day exploring and very late for dinner. They were both fairly sure they were going to be in trouble when they arrived.

Charlie looked over at his brother and saw he was worried. He knew just what to do! Henry loved ghost stories, and there was no better place to tell a scary story than by the spooky Flint River. He thought back to the summer before, when he and his brother went on a fishing trip with their grandpa. That night, as they sat around the campfire, their grandpa told many tales. One of those stories was about the Flint River. Hopefully, Henry would like the story, and it might keep his mind off how far they were from home.

"Hey, Henry," Charlie started, "do you remember that story grandpa told us about the Flint River last summer at the cabin?"

"No," said Henry, puzzled. "He must have told that one after I fell asleep. Is it good?"

"It is pretty good," smiled Charlie. Answering the question before Henry could answer it, he added "and definitely not TOO scary!"

Henry returned the smile. His brother knew him well.

"While I am telling you this story, be sure to be on the lookout for orbs. Remember? Orbs are those strange balls of light. People can see them but can't explain where they come from. They are supposed to be a sign that a spirit is present. I heard there are TONS of them along the banks of the river."

"Why are there so many spirits here?" asked Henry.

"Well," Charlie explained, "lots of people have died in the river. Some of them drowned. Some of them got swept away in the floods. And others...well, let's just say foul play was involved. So be on the lookout for orbs. I want to see one!"

"Me, too," said Henry, without much conviction. "I'll

look for orbs while you tell the story."

"Okay," Charlie began, "Grandpa said his favorite story about the river is the one about the apparition of a man who has appeared at dusk for more than 100 years! He only comes out at night. He can be seen near the Smith Street Bridge. Nowadays, we call it North Grand Traverse Street. "

"Aren't we pretty near there right now?" asked Henry.

Charlie looked around. His brother was right, they were close to the bridge. "Yep. We are not far away from it. Pay attention to the story!"

"Okay," Charlie continued. "The spirit walks along the river alone. He is searching the area."

"What is he looking for?" interrupted Henry.

"It's not what, it's WHO. When people see the man, he is moving his head back and forth, really looking. People call out to him, asking if he needs any help. He never answers."

"Why? It seems like if you lost something or some*one*, you'd want help finding it!" said Henry.

"Henry, if you don't stop interrupting, I am not going to tell the story," Charlie said.

"Fine. I am listening," Henry said while pretending to lock his lips with an imaginary key.

"Like I was saying, he never answers when people call out to him. Sometimes people get confused. They think that maybe he didn't hear them. So they walk toward him to offer their help. And this is where it gets weird. Once they get close to him, he disappears."

"Disappears?" asked Henry. "Like, poof? Gone?"

"Exactly," Charlie continued. "He disappears. Naturally, people started getting curious about the disappearing man, so they did a little research. It turns out, the man they have spotted on the river is a ghost. And he died in 1918!"

Henry kept his mouth closed, but his eyes widened. Charlie liked keeping his little brother in suspense.

"Way back in 1918, a man and a woman were on a date. They ate dinner together and then grabbed their ice skates to join some of their friends at a skating party near the Smith Street Bridge. They played Crack the Whip and all kinds of games. Everyone was having a good time. The man and woman skated away from the crowd so they could share a kiss in private. They passed over a piece of thin ice and fell into the river! Everyone started to panic. Their friends heard the loud crack of the ice and their shouts for help. By the time they skated over to them, it was too late."

"What do you mean, too late?" asked Henry.

"Too late to save them. They fell into the cold water, and the current carried them away. They were gone!"

"I still don't get it. How?"

"The Flint River is too deep and fast to fall all the way to the bottom of the river. Once they fell through the ice, they were in water that was moving as fast as it is right now! They were trapped under the ice and drowned."

"Whoa," replied Henry, imagining what it must be like to be trapped under the ice with no way to get out.

"Well, a few weeks later, they found the man's body, but they never found his girlfriend. They say the ghost of the man still roams the banks of the Flint River looking for his lost love."

"Not a bad story," said Henry. "But I have something a little better."

"What's that?" asked Charlie.

"Look over on the other side of the river," Henry pointed. Directly across from them, they spotted a man. And he appeared to be searching for something on the banks of the river.

Now that you've reached the end of the book, what do you think? Is Vehicle City REALLY a haunted city? Do ghosts lurk around Flint, or are these stories just eerie rumors?

Maybe the best way to find out is to conduct your own investigation. If you decide to do some ghost hunting to see if these spine-tingling tales are true, be careful! Ghosts that seem just a little bit spooky in the book might be TERRIFYING in real life! Remember to stay in groups, take notes, and always watch your back. You never know who—or what—might be right behind you!

Happy hunting!

Anna Lardinois tingles the spines of Milwaukee locals and visitors through her haunted, historical walking tours known as Gothic Milwaukee. The former English teacher is an ardent collector of stories, an avid walker and a sweet treat enthusiast. She happily resides in a historic home in Milwaukee that, at this time, does not appear to be haunted. Follow Anna on Twitter and at @gothicmilwaukee.

Check out some of the other Spooky America titles available now!

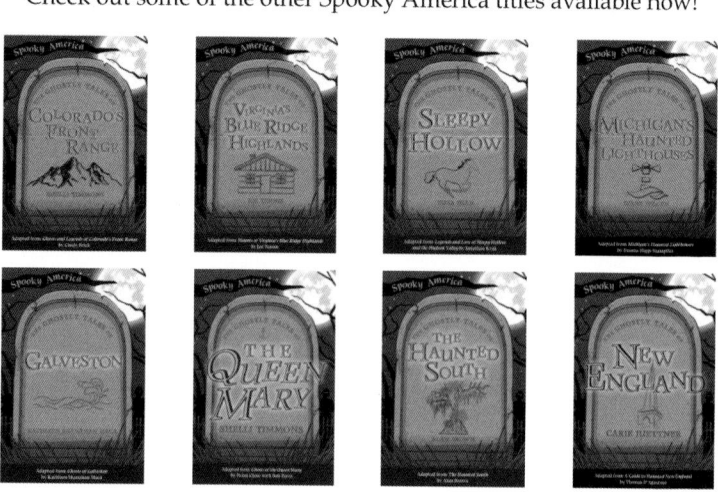

Spooky America was adapted from the creeptastic Haunted America series for adults. Haunted America explores historical haunts in cities and regions across America. Each book chronicles both the widely known and less-familiar history behind local ghosts and other unexplained mysteries. Here's more from *Haunted Flint* authors Roxanne Rhoads and Joe Schipani:

For more visit haunted-flint.com, or find them on Facebook @HauntedFlint.